# Somewhere a Tree waits for an Angel or a Butterfly

## Eileen Carney Hulme

First published 2024 by The Hedgehog Poetry Press

Published in the UK by
The Hedgehog Poetry Press
Coppack House, 5
Churchill Avenue
Clevedon
BS21 6QW

www.hedgehogpress.co.uk

ISBN: 978-1-916830-18-9

9 8 7 6 5 4 3 2 1

A CIP Catalogue record for this book is available from the British
Library.
Cover image *plum blossoms in moonlight* (18th century) vintage ink
and color on silk by Sō Shizan

# Contents

What's left behind ........................................................... 7

Lovers ............................................................................. 8

Somewhere a Tree waits for an Angel or a Butterfly........... 9

The Belt of Venus ........................................................... 10

Come here ...................................................................... 11

A Smudge of Love ......................................................... 12

Illusions ......................................................................... 13

Briefly ............................................................................ 14

If you could go anywhere ................................................ 15

Damp Shaped Us ........................................................... 16

Reverberations ............................................................... 17

Uncovering Truths.......................................................... 18

Sweet Time .................................................................... 19

Choosing a Stone ........................................................... 20

Afterlife.......................................................................... 21

When you wake............................................................... 22

Acknowledgements......................................................... 23

*Of time you would make a stream on whose bank you would sit and watch its flowing.*

Khalil Gibran

# What's left behind

I want the wind, wild
loosening my hair
gathering sea scents
a northern sky, so unpredictable
no one has found the right word
a frenzy of blues
thin strips of vermillion.
I am shaped by beach walks
by this night sky, a scatter
of stars you left behind
as whispered love words
unwithered.

# Lovers

The swifts came late
from their wintering grounds
keeping secret their routes
searching for dragonflies
building indoor nests.
You and I
blow as thistledown
wandering beachward
seeking the sea
where you tease
with your stone skimming
skills and spin me
towards incoming tide.
I laugh and scream
repeating your name
you respond with silence
lips finding the pale
shift of my throat.

# Somewhere a Tree waits for an Angel or a Butterfly

I reach inside my heart, remove
a handful of leaves
autumn gathered beneath
your shadow. Hieroglyphs
of small dreams, lost summers
the bend of clocks taking
the long road home. The way
you spoke their names –
*Copper Beech, Grey Willow, Silver Birch.*
My back to the bark I'm shaped
like loss, each little scar longing for wings.

# The Belt of Venus

Twice a day
the blue hour flirts
a lust for colour
a before or after red
or perhaps a scattering
of cosmic dust
making its way to earth
along a deserted path
that lovers seek.
Let's gather up that space
set it down over here
it's where we'll meet
in shadow-time
when everything surprises
where you and I
are reflections in a moving sky
high-wiring with the ease
of acrobats, startled
by an updraft of love.

# Come here

and I do
one step
I am leaves
to your branch

it is summer
sultry, a storm
is holding itself
out at sea

we are silent
this moment
has been long
in the making

let's not move
let's wait until
we taste rain
on our tongues.

# A Smudge of Love

I gather the flowers of youth
rose tints of spring
colours tie-dyed to the past
mind-door ajar
hearing words left unfinished

our small lives sea-tinged
where summer days melded
into flaming nights
believing only we could read the tides.

Like meadows of seagrass
I depend on light
forgive the storms
bruises of rain

whispering
this is how it was
a swift touch of sky
the bittersweet of daisies
...loves me, loves me not.

## Illusions

I never quite managed to remove
that red wine spot from
my white linen dress, perhaps
I didn't try hard enough.
A reminder of late night picnics
on a beach where the sky
hardly darkened in summer.
Does the dress still smell of wistful
a heady jasmine or a base note of sandalwood
a promise of no promises.
Last night I looked towards a shelf of light
in an otherwise clouded sky
I watched until it disappeared
not understanding how it got there
or why it was so slow to leave.

## Briefly

This is how small
a world can be
the opening or
closing of a door
a caught kiss
as it slips
through the dark
a need
to remember hands
their shape
the time it takes
to pull me close
and the pulse
of rain, unnerved
by all that blue.

# If you could go anywhere

Where would you go?
With the curtains open
stars are our astral guides,
night lights of protection,
they hear our conversations
keep our secrets.

We talk of countries,
distances that hold no fear.
Your hands map a journey
along my spine, cartography
of love spells that wing
as itinerant fireflies.

Where would you go?
you ask again.

Here, I say
knowing there is
nothing beyond.

## Damp Shaped Us

It was always about the rain
more or less. A mash-up
of mid-clouds revealing
their characters, traits of
each zodiac sign. Here
everything is weathered
hollow of beach huts
salt-crusted scents
blowing inland.
And when stars fell we were
there to catch them. We kept
them in pockets, inside books
only took them out if it rained
held them as charms
against ragged skies.

# Reverberations

I hurry to the beach
find the waves receptive
to my changing moods

here
the sky hugs
with its dipping cloud cover
allows a pain to heal
sorrow to abate.

Remember
how we would chase
waves, chase the light
and you would whisper secrets
to a shell
and I would hold it to my ear.

The air made thin, I listen still
hoping to hear those missing words.

## Uncovering Truths

Stones gather here
and driftwood and bones
you are wearing your black
shirt with its mad flowers.
I feel naked
this is how
it is to love.
Fear is a weathervane
an arrow that turns
and you have no control.
But for now
we are East
scrying this beach
with its residue of karma.
Dipping into the cold
North Sea, the breeze
loans us direction.

# Sweet Time

i.

and your shadow
comes to meet me
on the sun-side
here hands play
light and dark
you pull me to you
and everything's a
perfect fit
as scents collide
absorb then diffuse

ii.

there's a stillness
when eyes shape
a question
and before
an answer
then a rollercoaster
ride, as dangerous
to remain
as jumping off

iii.

someone is making
*A Clock of the Long Now*
that ticks once a year
let's wrap ourselves
in sky and kiss
until earth catches up.

## Choosing a Stone

What would you say to me
now, that I looked too closely
at the moon and when my heart
quickened did you bend
to kiss me, unfolding stars
that leapt from the sky
during a cloudburst,
their fate undecided.

Listen, nothing matters
the breeze through
marram grass carries our love
and in the sometime
that was never our time
you will still skim stones
and turn to me
with your half smile.

# Afterlife

I do not think of you
as gone, that winged word
like a kiss on the cheek
wave of a hand.
I think of you
as somewhere else
new, unknown
waking to blue
stretching to greet
the ocean, laughing
with stars.
One is named after you
I seek it out at night
I say come find me
in the here and now
in all tomorrows.

I do not think of you as gone.

## When you wake

From a dream, confusion
time is lost or hidden.
Dust motes hover in the half
light and you move to the cold
side as the house settles itself
around you and the often heard
creak in the hall breathes out.
At first you found it frightening
then reassuring, now it's another
reminder not to listen for
the gate off the latch
the key in the lock.

Death is silent
and all the ghosts are at play.

## Acknowledgements

My thanks to the many editors who have published my work, some of the poems appear in this book. I am especially grateful to the wonderful Indigo Dreams for regularly featuring my poems in their magazines, for publishing my 2$^{nd}$ and 3$^{rd}$ collections, Ronnie as poetry editor of my 1$^{st}$ with Bluechrome.

Special thanks to Alison Lock, Bren Booth-Jones and Mike Fox for their generous words.

Mark Davidson, much gratitude to you for liking my poems enough to award me some prizes and for choosing this selection as a winning entry of The Crimson Spine inaugural competition. It's a real pleasure to be a Hedgehog Poetry author.

"The night sky of the far north is 'hardly darkened' on a stilled summer's evening while the storms are held out at sea. We are secure in the depths, holding our breath, hushed by the touch of pen on paper. These words are tinctures, the essence of landscape in drops of ink on a page, words that leave us lasting impressions of love in all its whispered secrets. Here you will find tenderness in the longing and the agelessness of love."

Alison Lock, poet

"Eileen Carney Hulme's new collection is a beautiful and atmospheric arrangement of subtle and bittersweet melodies. She captures the pathos and specificity of 'small lives sea-tinged' and 'beach huts / salt-crusted' with marvellous sensitivity and insight, yet she amplifies these details effortlessly into larger themes and questions. Carney Hulme's poems braid wistfulness and hope. They truly are 'charms against ragged skies'."

Bren Booth-Jones, author of *Blue Remembered Star*

"Distilled and deeply crafted as Eileen's poems are, I find in them a free-spiritedness and non –conformity which belies expectation based on what one might have read before. Characteristic also is a strong transpersonal element, a sense of larger forces at play, so that the intensely personal might be contextualised by the ambience of the natural world, the present moment by a sense of the passage of time."

Mike Fox, author